FUN WITH CHEMISTRY

New Revised Edition

FUN WITH CHEMISTRY

by MAE and IRA FREEMAN

Edited by L. H. ANGUS, M.Sc., F.R.I.C.

KAYE & WARD LTD.   *LONDON*

Copyright, 1944, 1962, by Random House Inc.,
except as defined below

Copyright © 1961, 1967, Edmund Ward (Publishers)
Limited in the case of the revised text pages 12, 14,
18, 22, 44 and 48 and photographs pages 15, 18, 23,
25, 27, 37, 39, 43, 45 (lower), 47, 49 (upper), 51 (lower)
and 55

First published in Great Britain by
EDMUND WARD (PUBLISHERS) LIMITED
194 Bishopsgate, London, EC2
1961

Revised edition by
EDMUND WARD (PUBLISHERS) LIMITED
1967

Reprinted by
KAYE & WARD LIMITED
194-200 Bishopsgate, London EC2
1971

All rights reserved. No part of this publication may be reproduced, stored in a
retrieval system, or transmitted, in any form or by any means, electronic,
mechanical, photocopying, recording or otherwise, without the prior permission
of the copyright owner

ISBN 0 7182 0055 1

Printed Offset in England by
STRAKER BROTHERS, LIMITED
London

CONTENTS

Charles Goodyear happened to drop a piece of raw rubber mixed with sulphur on a hot stove. That is how he discovered a way of making rubber stronger and more elastic. He called it *vulcanized* rubber. Almost all the rubber used these days is vulcanized.

WHAT CHEMISTRY IS ABOUT

Look around you right now and notice how many different materials there are in your room. There may be a table made of wood, a doorknob made of brass, a piece of chalk, and a glass window. There may be paper, cloth, plastics and many other materials.

The chemist studies different materials such as these and nearly a million others. He learns what things are made of and finds out how to make new materials by putting well-known ones together in different ways. The chemist makes vitamins and drugs to keep people healthy. He discovers how to make new kinds of cloth from coal, water and air. He helps make the world brighter, safer and more comfortable with gleaming plastics and useful new metals.

The science of chemistry started only about two hundred years ago. Before that, experimenters worked mainly at trying to make gold out of iron or other ordinary metals. Although they never found how to do this, they learned some things about materials which made them curious and led them on.

Gradually, chemistry became a real science as people found out more about materials and what they are made of. It was not until about fifty years ago that things made through chemistry became an important part of modern life.

This book will show you how chemists get some of their amazing results. The best way to see this is by trying some interesting experiments that you can do at home. If you follow the instructions carefully, none of the experiments will be dangerous or messy.

The materials you will use in your laboratory work can be found in the kitchen, laundry or medicine cabinet. All you will need to buy are two or three test tubes which you can get at the chemists.

If an experiment does not work the first time you do it, check the instructions carefully and try it again.

MAKING AND USING
A TEST-TUBE HOLDER

In some of your chemical experiments, you will need a test-tube holder. This is used to hold the tube while it is being heated over a candle flame.

Get a coat hanger made of thin wire and untwist the ends where they are joined. Cut off a piece about a foot long. You can do this by snipping it with the cutting part of a pair of pliers. Or you can hold the wire with the pliers and bend it back and forth until it breaks.

Now find a piece of pipe or a round stick of wood which is about the same size as your test tubes. Hold one end of the wire firmly against the stick with the pliers, and bend it around the stick two or three times, as shown in the picture. Slip the wire off, and bend the other end into a loop to form a handle. Try one of the test tubes in the holder. Adjust the turns of wire so that the tube goes in easily but does not fall through.

When you heat something in a test tube, always hold the tube at a slant so that the candle flame is under the *side* of the tube, near the bottom. Always point the open end of the tube off to one side, away from your own and anyone else's face, in case the liquid should spatter.

The candle used for heating should be set firmly in a candlestick, or it can be stuck onto a metal jar lid with a drop of melted candle wax.

You must be very careful when you do any experiment in which a candle is used. The best place to work is on a metal table or alongside a sink. Be sure to keep the flame away from curtains or anything else that could catch fire easily.

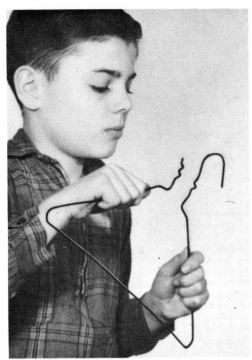

Untwist the ends . . .

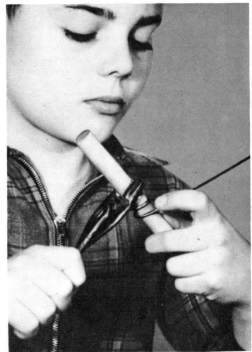

bend the wire around a stick . . .

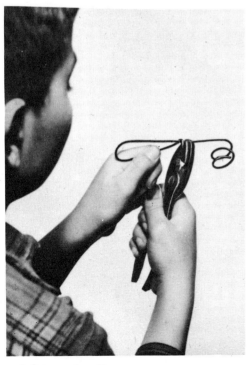

and form a handle.

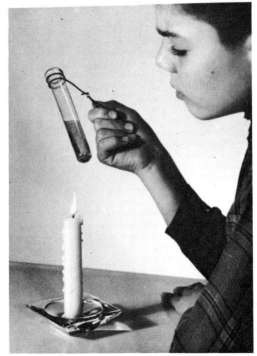

Using the holder.

MORE THINGS TO MAKE

To hold test tubes straight up while you work, you will need a test-tube rack. Make one by cutting away the side of a small cardboard box, such as a sugar carton. Then cut three or four holes in the top, each one just big enough to hold a test tube.

When you use a powder in an experiment, dump what you need onto a piece of stiff paper that has been creased down the middle. Then you can easily pour the powder into a glass or test tube.

Another useful thing to have in your home laboratory is a measuring glass. You can make one by sticking a strip of adhesive tape down the side of a small glass. Divide the length of the strip into four equal parts and mark them as shown in the picture.

Make a funnel for pouring liquids into a test tube. Cut a six-inch square of either wax paper or aluminium foil. Fold it in half each way, as shown in the picture. Snip off the very tip of the folded corner. Then open out the paper to form a cone, so that there are three thicknesses of paper on one side and one thickness on the other. Your funnel is now ready to use.

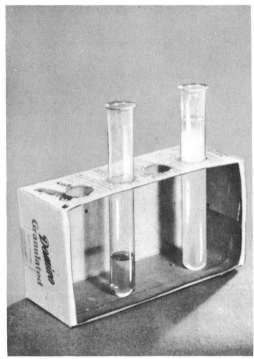

Test tube rack.

How to pour a powder.

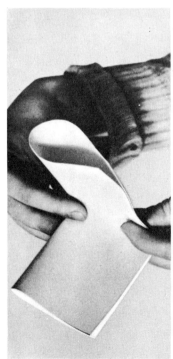

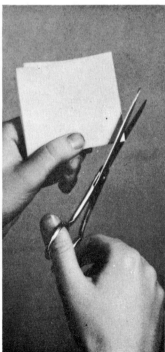

Fold it in half.

Snip off the tip.

Using the funnel.

ATOMS AND MOLECULES

Scientists know that every kind of material is made of very tiny specks called MOLECULES. Molecules are far too small to be seen, even with the strongest microscope. A hundred million molecules, side by side, would make a row only an inch long!

Between the molecules there are spaces. This means that everything that seems quite solid really has holes all through it. The holes are the empty places between the molecules.

Do an experiment to show that there really can be spaces in something that does not seem to have any.

Fill a small glass with pieces of cotton wool. Fill another glass with water. If you are careful and do it slowly, you can pour the whole glass of water into the glass already full of cotton wool. Then you have two glasses of material in only one glass.

Each separate kind of material is made up of molecules that are all alike. For example, water has its own special kind of molecules. So has salt, and chalk, and every other material in the world.

Molecules are made up of even smaller specks called ATOMS. A material that has *only one kind* of atom in its molecules is called a chemical ELEMENT. A material that has *more than one kind* of atom in its molecules is called a chemical COMPOUND.

There are only about a hundred different elements, but their atoms can hook together in very many different ways to form molecules of compounds. Chemists know about a million different compounds, and all of them are made from only the hundred elements.

Most elements are known only to scientists, but some of the things you see every day are made of materials that are chemical elements. There are IRON nails, ALUMINIUM pots and SILVER spoons. The black part of a burnt match is CARBON. A tin can is made of iron covered with a thin layer of the element TIN.

Chemists sometimes make models of molecules to study how the atoms are put together. The lower picture shows a model of a molecule of aspirin, which is a compound of three elements. The coloured balls stand for the three different kinds of atoms.

6

Two glasses of material go into one glass.

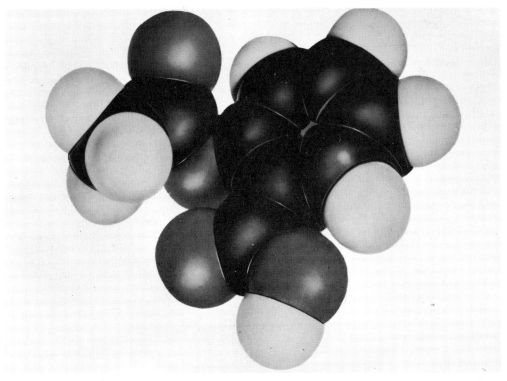
A molecule model.

CRYSTALS OF SUGAR

When sugar is stirred into water, the grains get smaller and smaller until you cannot see them any more. That is because the water makes the sugar divide into separate molecules. The sugar molecules spread out among the water molecules.

Any material that breaks up and spreads through a liquid in this way is DISSOLVED. The dissolved sugar is still there even though it is invisible, and you can get it back again.

Put a glass of water into a pan and heat it on the stove. When the water begins to boil, turn the flame low and stir sugar into the water little by little. Keep adding sugar slowly until no more will dissolve. This may take two or three cups of sugar. Pour the mixture into a glass.

Tie a short piece of cotton string to a pencil. The length of the string should be about the same as the height of the glass. Tie a button or a paper clip to the bottom end of the string, so that it will hang straight down. Now lower the string into the liquid, letting the pencil rest across the top of the glass. Set the glass away in a warm place.

After a few days, you will see that the string is covered with small bits of frosty-looking material. These bits are CRYSTALS of sugar.

Crystals are many-sided pieces that form when any dissolved solid material comes out of a liquid again.

When your sugar liquid cooled, it could no longer hold all of the dissolved sugar. It had to give some of it up in the form of crystals. If the liquid cools very slowly, the crystals will be large.

Crystals of sugar sometimes form in a jar of jam or honey that has been standing for a long time.

Lift out the crystals of sugar.

MORE ABOUT CRYSTALS

The crystals of different materials have different shapes. A chemist can often recognize a material by the form of its crystals.

Spread a few grains of table salt on a piece of paper and look at them with a magnifying lens. You will see that each crystal is a perfect little cube.

In winter, let a snowflake land on your woollen glove or sleeve. Then look at it with a magnifying lens. Notice that it has a regular shape, with six sides. When water turns into ice or snow, it always forms six-sided crystals. Snowflakes are made up of such crystals, and so they always have six sides or points.

Many materials found in the earth, such as valuable gems, have crystals with special shapes. They formed a very long time ago, when the melted materials inside the earth began to cool. A diamond is just a crystal of carbon. An interesting experiment will show you some crystals of an unusual shape.

Get a small amount of MAGNESIUM SULPHATE from your medicine cabinet or at the chemists. This is a compound that is usually called Epsom salts.

Put a quarter of a glass of water into a small pan and heat it on the stove. Stir in Epsom salts until no more will dissolve. This may take three or four teaspoons of crystals.

Remove the pan from the stove and add one or two drops of liquid glue. Stir until the glue has all dissolved. Now, with a wad of cotton wool, spread some of the mixture evenly onto a piece of glass.

In a few minutes, needle-like crystals will begin to appear in the liquid. You can actually watch them grow out in all directions. Soon the whole piece of glass will be covered with a pretty, frost-like pattern. When the water dries completely, you will have a good sample of magnesium sulphate crystals.

Spread the mixture onto a piece of glass.

The crystals look like frost on a window.

WATER FROM CRYSTALS

Some crystals seem perfectly dry, but they may have water locked up chemically inside them. An example of this is ordinary washing soda, which chemists call SODIUM CARBONATE. Here is a way to get the water out of this compound.

Take a lump of washing soda and wipe it briskly with a cloth to rub off the powder that covers it. Notice that the cleaned piece is clear and crystal-like. Break up this lump so that you can put it into a clean test tube.

Heat the tube gently by holding it an inch or two above a candle flame. In a short time, the pieces of soda will become wet. This moisture will steam up with crackling sounds. When the steam reaches the cool upper part of the tube it will turn to water again, forming drops on the glass. Soon only a dry, white powder will be left in the bottom of the tube. Be careful to prevent any of the condensed water running back onto the hot glass, otherwise your tube may crack.

The pieces you started with seemed perfectly dry. Where did the water come from? Each molecule of sodium carbonate in a crystal has ten molecules of water hooked up with it chemically. You cannot by appearance tell that any water is there because it forms part of the solid crystal. But when the crystals are heated, the water molecules come loose. They gather to form drops that you can see.

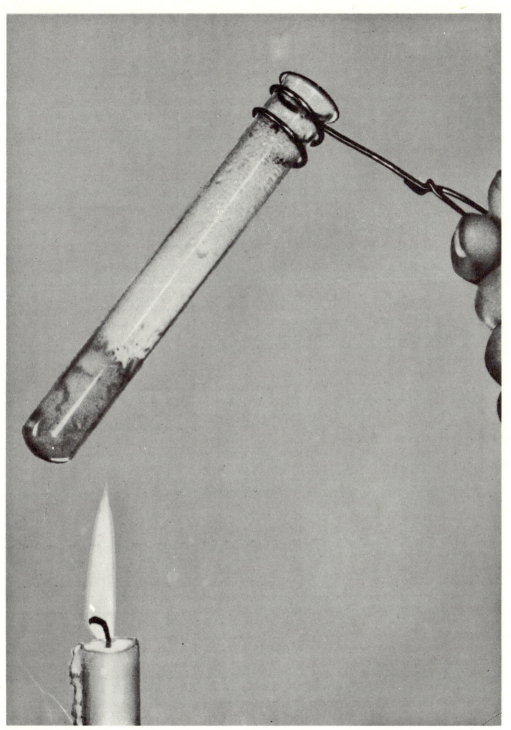

Drops of water form in the upper part of the tube.

THE CHEMISTRY OF FIRE

After a piece of paper or wood has burned up, there is only a little black crust left. For a long time, people believed that some strange, invisible material came out of anything that burned. Later, they found that what really happens is just the opposite. The thing that burns takes up something from the air around it.

Air is a cloud of separate molecules. Any such cloud of molecules is called a GAS. Air is a mixture of different gases, and one of them is a chemical element called OXYGEN.

When any material burns, it hooks up chemically with oxygen to form some new compounds. Most of these compounds are gases, which float away. That is why there seems to be almost nothing left afterward.

Oxygen has no colour, no taste, no smell. You cannot see it. But without this gas, no fire could burn and no animal could breathe. The oxygen that you take into your lungs when you breathe joins up with waste materials in your body. It really burns them away. So breathing is just a slow kind of burning.

You can easily see how oxygen is taken up in burning by trying an experiment.

Stick a short length of candle to the bottom of a dish with a drop or two of melted wax. Put some water in the dish and light the candle. Hold a tall glass with its open end down, and lower it over the candle.

Let the glass stand there with its edge under water, and watch what happens. The water rises slowly inside the glass. Finally, the flame dies out.

When the candle wax burned, some of the elements in it joined chemically with oxygen from the air inside the glass. The compounds that formed took up less room than the oxygen did before. This made more room inside the glass, so the outside air pushed some water in. After a short time, there was not enough oxygen left to keep the flame going. In this experiment some of the rise of water was due to heated air escaping from the glass and water rising to replace this air when the apparatus cooled after the candle flame had been extinguished. To show that some oxygen has been used get a second glass of the same size and hold it over the candle flame for the air to become heated. Then place this glass into a second dish containing water but no candle. As the air cools water will rise but not as high as in the first dish.

Besides oxygen, air is made up mainly of another gas called NITROGEN. This gas usually does not take part in chemical actions, so it has nothing to do with burning.

Put the glass over the candle.

Water goes up into the glass.

CANDLE CHEMISTRY

The last experiment showed that a candle, like anything else, needs oxygen when it burns. Many things happen to a burning candle. The flame is really a small chemistry laboratory.

When you light a candle, some wax melts. The liquid wax spreads up through the wick. Then the heat of the flame changes the melted wax to a gas. This gas burns and gives out light and heat. If you blow the flame out, a smoky streak keeps rising from the wick. This smoke comes from the gas that has not yet burned, and it is changing back to tiny drops of wax. Try an experiment to show that these drops will still burn.

Light a candle with a kitchen match. Then hold the burning match off to one side as you blow out the candle with a quick puff. As soon as you see smoke coming from the wick, bring the match flame into the trail of smoke an inch or two above the candle. The flame jumps downward and lights the wick again.

Candle wax is made up of compounds that have the element CARBON in them. When the wax molecules break up in the hot flame, little specks of black carbon are set free. The heat of the flame gives them a yellow glow. That is how the candle sends out light.

To catch these black carbon specks, take a small strip of aluminium foil and fold it down the middle to make it stiff. Hold one end of the foil in the flame for a few seconds. When you take it out you will see the black smudge that was left when some of the carbon atoms stuck to the metal.

Another element in candle wax is HYDROGEN. The wax molecules break down in the flame and hydrogen atoms come off. When the hydrogen atoms get to the outside part of the flame, they join with oxygen atoms from the air. Can you guess what compound is formed? Try this experiment and see:

Hold a cold glass upside down over the candle flame for a second or two. Then rub your finger over the mist that forms on the glass. It is water.

Petrol is made up of compounds of hydrogen and carbon. Most of the carbon burns up in the engine to form two gases–CARBON MONOXIDE and CARBON DIOXIDE (see page 36). Carbon monoxide is very poisonous, even if you breathe only a tiny bit of it. That is why a car engine should never be run in a closed garage.

A black smudge forms.

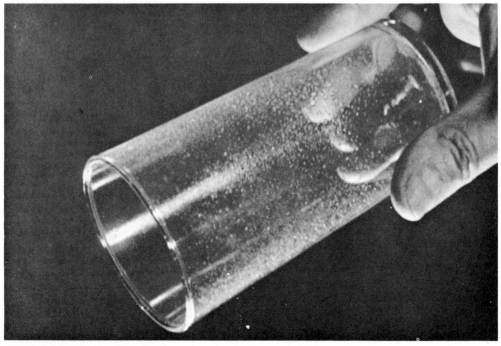

Moisture gathers inside the glass.

USING OXYGEN

Oxygen is all around us, not only in the air but in many compounds. The oxygen needed to make things burn usually comes from the air. Another way to get oxygen is to take it out of one of its compounds.

Nearly half of the solid earth is made up of oxygen, and water is almost all oxygen. It is not easy to get this element out of these compounds, but there are some other compounds where it can be done. You can use one in an experiment.

Get a small bottle of HYDROGEN PEROXIDE at the chemists. There may be one in your medicine cabinet at home. Pour about an inch of this liquid into a test tube and stand it in your test-tube rack. Get a very thin strip of wood or a broom straw (NOT the plastic kind). Light a candle and have it handy nearby.

Everything in this experiment must be done quickly. Put a few drops of laundry bleach into the peroxide. It will foam and sizzle. Hold one end of the straw in the candle flame. When it catches fire, let the straw burn for a second or two and then blow out the flame. The end will keep glowing.

Quickly stick the end of the glowing straw into the test tube, just above the liquid. It will burst into bright flame again with a sharp, popping noise. Shake the tube a few times and the liquid will foam up once more. Then try the glowing straw again.

The test showed that things burn faster in pure oxygen than in air, where the oxygen is mixed with other gases.

Hydrogen peroxide is a compound. Each molecule has two hydrogen atoms and two oxygen atoms in it. In your experiment, you added some bleach to the hydrogen peroxide. This helped one oxygen atom get loose from each hydrogen peroxide molecule. Then all the oxygen atoms that were set free in this way made the straw flame up again.

Pure oxygen is sometimes made in large amounts by running an electrical current through water (see page 54). Then the gas is stored in strong steel tanks. Other gases can be mixed with it and burned to give a flame hot enough to cut steel easily. Oxygen is also used for burning carbon out of iron in order to change it to steel.

The engines of some rockets get their oxygen from hydrogen peroxide. Long-range rockets carry along oxygen that has been turned to a liquid at a temperature of 300 degrees below zero.

The glowing straw bursts into flame.

The rocket engine uses oxygen from hydrogen peroxide.

BURNING SUGAR

Sugar is a chemical compound that is made up of three elements. They are carbon, oxygen and hydrogen.

. Carbon is a smudgy, black solid material. Oxygen and hydrogen are invisible gases. But when these three elements join chemically, they can form sweet, white crystals of sugar.

You can burn a lump of sugar to break down its molecules, but the burning must be done in a special way.

Twist a piece of thin wire around a lump of sugar. Use the wire as a handle and hold one corner of the lump in a candle flame. The sugar will not actually burn. It may blacken a little and even begin to melt, but the molecules will not break down. The black smudge is only carbon from the candle flame and not from the sugar molecules.

Now put a speck of cigarette ash on a fresh corner of the sugar lump. Hold this corner in the edge of the flame. In a second or two, the sugar will begin to burn with a blue flame, bubbling and spouting out little smoke rings.

A shiny black mass will drip down as the sugar burns. This has carbon atoms in it that are set free when the sugar molecules break up. The hydrogen and oxygen atoms form other compounds that go off into the air.

Have a dish handy to catch any drops that melt off. Be careful not to let any hot sugar drip onto your hand.

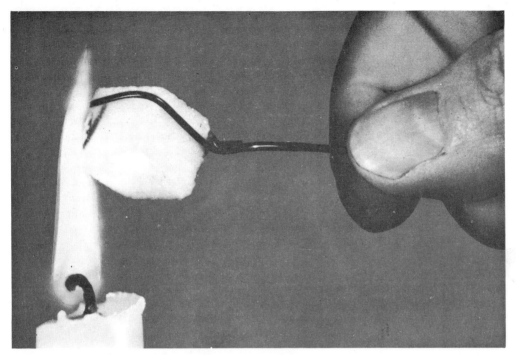

Touch the corner of the sugar lump to the flame.

Smoke rings shoot out.

INVISIBLE WRITING

On page 14 you found out that breathing is a slow kind of burning. There are other chemical changes where oxygen hooks up with a material so slowly that there is no smoke or flame. You can watch this happen in an experiment with secret writing.

Dip a clean pen into some lemon juice and write something on a sheet of heavy writing paper. Dip the pen often, so you can make a good, heavy line. The liquid will soon dry and leave no mark.

Set up a lighted candle in a sink. For safety, this is the best place to do the experiment.

Now hold the paper an inch or so above the candle flame, keeping the paper moving all the time. Do not hold it still or it may catch fire. Soon you can see the writing, traced in dark brown lines.

Wherever you put lemon juice on the paper, it was changed chemically. It became a compound that burns more easily than the rest of the paper. When the paper was heated, the prepared part was the first to turn brown.

Try the same experiment by writing with grapefruit juice or milk. They work as well as lemon juice.

Above: Write with a heavy line.
Below: Heat brings out the writing.

BLEACHING WITH OXYGEN

The bleaching of clothes in the laundry is another example of a chemical change that uses oxygen. That means that bleaching is also a slow kind of burning. And this time the burning even takes place under water!

A laundry bleach is a compound that whitens clothes by giving off oxygen. This oxygen joins chemically with the materials that soil or discolour the cloth. It changes them to new compounds that are lighter in colour or have no colour at all. See how this works by doing an experiment.

Stir a few drops of ink into half a glass of water to make a fairly dark blue mixture. Pour in a few drops of laundry bleach and stir again. The dark colour will quickly fade away and the liquid will become almost completely clear. The dye in the ink loses its colour when it hooks up with oxygen from the bleach.

Bleaching is an important step in making cotton cloth because the natural cotton is not perfectly white. Paper, straw, linen and many other materials are made white by bleaching.

The ink loses its colour.

RUSTING OF IRON

There is another kind of burning that goes even slower than bleaching. It is the rusting of iron or steel.

Whenever air and water touch iron, brown flakes of rust are formed. The rust is a chemical compound made up of iron, oxygen from the air, and water. All three of these materials are needed to form rust. Find out how this happens by doing an experiment.

Pull a few small tufts of steel wool off a pad like the ones used for cleaning pots and pans. If there is soap on the metal, shake it off as well as you can. Wet the steel wool and push it into the bottom of a test tube.

Put half an inch of water in a glass and stand the tube upside down in it. After a day or two, notice that water has gone up into the tube, just as in the experiment with the burning candle on page 16.

The reason the water rises is the same in both experiments. Some oxygen has been taken out of the air, this time by the iron. In the test with the candle, everything happened in a few moments. With rusting, the chemical change takes a long time.

Look closely at the steel wool and you will see brown spots of rust.

Many years ago, chemists did a famous experiment with rusting. They carefully weighed a piece of iron. Then they let it rust and weighed it again. This time, the piece of iron weighed a little *more* than before. Something had been added to the iron. This extra material turned out to be oxygen that the iron took from the air as it rusted.

Rust is flaky and weak. That is why it is important to protect bridges, buildings, ships and other things made of steel. This is usually done by covering the steel with paint or with a layer of some other metal.

As the steel rusts, the water rises.

BURNING STEEL

In the last experiment, iron joined with oxygen very slowly when it rusted. But iron can burn rapidly, too. You cannot set fire to a large piece of iron or steel, but very thin strips of the metal can be made to burn. That is because oxygen from the air can get to the metal more easily when it is in small pieces.

Pull a tuft of steel wool from a pot-cleaning pad. Shake off most of the soap and twist one end of the tuft tightly onto a small stick. Spread out the loose ends.

Set up a lighted candle in a sink. Touch the tuft to the candle flame. When the steel strips begin to sputter, pull the tuft out of the flame and watch it burn. It will crackle and spark, and little drops of burning metal will fall into the sink. You can see one of these drops in the picture.

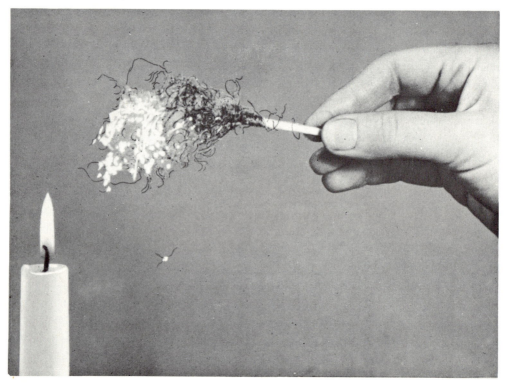

Steel can burn when it is in thin strips.

IODINE AND STARCH

Get a small bottle of **TINCTURE OF IODINE** from your medicine cabinet or at the chemists. Stir a teaspoon of flour into a small glass half full of hot water. Allow it to cool and then let one or two drops of iodine fall into the glass. The liquid will turn dark blue.

You have just made a test that chemists use to see if there is starch in a material. Starch is found in many plants. Its molecules are made up of carbon, hydrogen and oxygen atoms. Sugar is made up of the same three elements. But they are put together in a different way, and that makes sugar and starch very different from each other.

Whenever iodine touches anything that has starch in it, the mixture turns blue. Your test shows that flour has starch in it.

Try a drop of iodine on small bits of mashed potato, spaghetti, apple, cereal and sugar to see which of these have starch in them.

Testing for starch.

STARCH FROM POTATOES

Potatoes have much starch in them. Here is a way to get some of this starch out so you can use it in an experiment.

Peel and grate two large potatoes. Gather the corners of a handkerchief to make a bag and put the grated potato into it. Dip this bag into a bowl half full of water, lift it out and squeeze it, as the picture shows. Do this several times. The water will get cloudy.

Let the water stand for a few minutes and a white material will settle in the bottom of the bowl. Carefully pour off as much of the clear water as you can. Then set the bowl aside until the rest of the water dries away.

The white powder that is left is starch. Test a little of it with a drop of iodine, and save the rest for the next experiment.

Starch is a material that has many uses. It is a food that gives you energy. There are large amounts of starch in such foods as corn, wheat, rye, rice and potatoes. Before your body can use this starch, it must change it chemically to a kind of sugar.

In the laundry, starch is put onto shirts and dresses to make the cloth smooth. Starch is also used in making paper, glue, explosives and many other things.

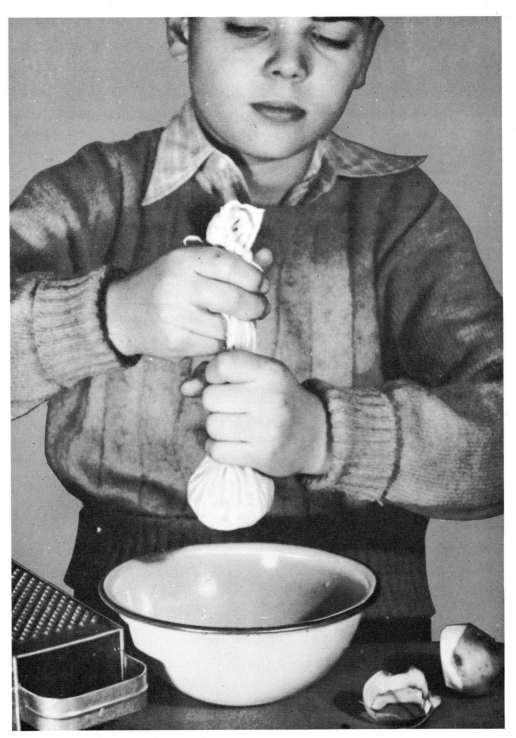

Squeeze the bag to get the starch out.

CLOUDY LIQUIDS

In the experiment on page 8, you saw how sugar can dissolve in water to form a clear liquid. But if starch is mixed with water, it does not dissolve, and the liquid is cloudy. Starch does not break up into separate molecules in water, as sugar does. Instead, it breaks up into tiny grains. These grains are too small to see, but they are very much bigger than molecules.

Do an experiment with light that will show that starch really does not dissolve in water.

Pour about half a glass of water into a small pan. Add a teaspoon of the potato starch you made in the last experiment. Heat the mixture over a low flame while stirring it with a spoon. When the starch comes to a boil, it will form a jelly-like paste.

Stir a few drops of this paste into a fresh glass of water. The starch seems to disappear, but you can test it and see that it really has not dissolved.

Cut a small hole in a piece of cardboard and hold it between a bright lamp and the glass of starch water, as in the picture. The starch grains catch the light and spread it in all directions. That is why you see the beam of light where it goes through the liquid.

You can make the same test using a glass of water with sugar dissolved in it. This time the beam will go right through and you will hardly be able to see it. That is because the separate sugar molecules are too small to catch the light and spread it.

Any material that does not settle out of a liquid is called a COLLOID. Your blood is a colloid; so is ice cream. Colloids are important in making paint, rubber, cement and many other things.

You can see the light in the liquid.

FLAME TESTS

Chemists have worked out many ways to test materials and find out what elements are in them. One way is to put a bit of the material in a flame and notice the colours that come from it.

Wet the clean end of a used wooden match stick and dip it into some table salt. Put the end with the salt on it into a small gas flame. All at once, the flame will turn a bright yellow. This colour tells the chemist that an element called SODIUM is in the material being tested.

Salt is a compound that has sodium in it. Sodium shows up so easily in a flame test that just one crystal of salt would be enough to colour a million gas flames.

For the next test, take another used match stick. Wet one end and dip it into some cream of tartar, which is used in baking. When you put this material into the gas flame, tiny red sparks stream off, as in the picture. This red colour shows that the element POTASSIUM is there.

Now get some boric acid from the medicine cabinet and do a flame test with it. The green colour of the flame means that the element of BORON is in the material.

Chemists also work with an instrument called a SPECTROSCOPE. The material to be tested is heated until it glows. The different colours in the light are sorted out by the spectroscope. From this, the chemist can tell which elements are in the material.

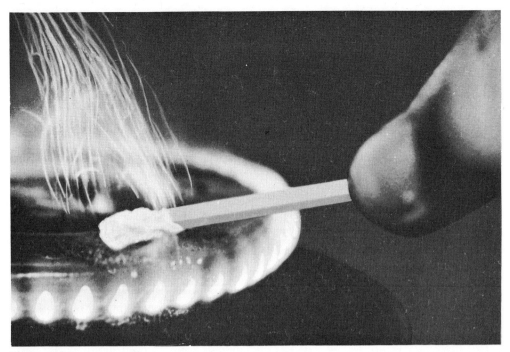

Red sparks stream off.

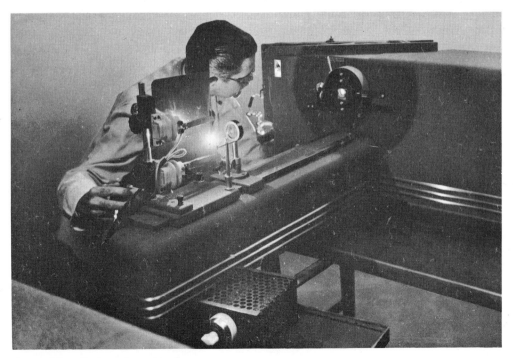

A machine that sorts out colours.

MAKING CARBON DIOXIDE

When a charge of gunpowder or dynamite is exploded, great amounts of gas are suddenly set free. The gases rush out with a crashing noise, and the force of the explosion can cause much damage.

But where was all this gas before the charge was fired? It was locked up chemically in the solid material until it was let loose. Set off a small, harmless explosion to see how such chemical actions work.

Get a large bottle and a cork that fits it well. Put about two tablespoons of baking soda on a small, creased piece of paper. Slide the powder into the bottle. Get ready a test tube full of vinegar. Moisten the cork with water.

Now be ready to work quickly. Hold the wet cork in one hand and the test tube of vinegar in the other. Pour the vinegar into the bottle and immediately cork it, but not too tightly.

The materials in the bottle will fizz and bubble, and after a moment the cork will blow into the air with a loud pop.

Baking soda is the household name for the chemical compound SODIUM BICARBONATE. It is made up of the elements sodium, hydrogen, carbon and oxygen. When vinegar is mixed with this compound, the chemical action sets free a gas called CARBON DIOXIDE. This gas builds up inside the bottle and finally blows the cork out.

Carbon dioxide is a compound of carbon and oxygen. These atoms were part of the sodium bicarbonate molecules and were set free by the vinegar.

Carbon dioxide is usually a gas, as it was in your experiment, but it can be made to form solid crystals. Then it is called 'dry ice,' and its temperature is over a hundred degrees below zero!

Suddenly the cork blows out.

THE GAS IN A SODA

Here is another experiment with carbon dioxide:

Pour a tablespoon of vinegar into a glass of water and add a tablespoon of baking soda. Drop three moth balls into the glass.

Soon you will see many tiny bubbles of carbon dioxide forming on the moth balls. The bubbles of gas act like little floats and make each moth ball rise to the top of the liquid. Then some of the bubbles break off and the ball slowly sinks. More bubbles begin to gather and the ball rises again.

Watch the three moth balls as they keep going up and down. This may go on for several hours, until all the chemicals are used up.

Notice that there are some bubbles all through the liquid, but they form more easily on the rough sides of the moth balls.

The rising bubbles make the liquid look like a glass of soda. Bottled soda drinks are made by forcing carbon dioxide gas into water that has sugar and flavouring in it. The gas is really dissolved in the water. When you open the bottle, the carbon dioxide shows up as small bubbles all through the liquid. These gas bubbles give the drink its sparkling taste.

Gas bubbles lift the moth balls.

THE GAS THAT CHOKES FIRE

Light a wooden kitchen match and hold it just inside the opening of a milk bottle or jar. It will keep on burning because it can get the oxygen it needs from the air around it.

Now put a tablespoon of baking soda into the bottle and pour in about a quarter of a glass of vinegar. The carbon dioxide that is set free gradually fills the bottle, pushing out the air that was there before. By the time the foaming stops, the bottle is filled with carbon dioxide gas, which stays inside just as water would.

Make the test with the lighted match again. This time the match will go out as soon as you put it in the opening of the bottle.

When the flame was dipped into the carbon dioxide, it had to go out because it could no longer get air to keep it burning.

Your experiment showed that carbon dioxide gas is heavier than air. It did not float upward but stayed down in the bottle. You can do another experiment to prove that this gas can be poured from one jar to another, just like a liquid.

Set a short stub of candle inside a small jar and light it. Be sure the candle is not as tall as the jar.

Make a bottle full of carbon dioxide gas as you did in the above experiment. As soon as the strong foaming stops, *pour the gas* gently from the bottle into the small jar, just as if you were pouring water. Take care that none of the vinegar comes out too.

Although you cannot see it, the carbon dioxide will fill the jar. As soon as it reaches the wick, the flame will go out.

Nothing can burn in carbon dioxide. That makes this gas a good fire fighter. Many of the fire extinguishers you see in schools and other buildings contain carbon dioxide. The gas is mixed with a soapy liquid. This makes a foam that can be sprayed onto the fire to put it out.

The match burns in air.

Carbon dioxide puts it out.

CHANGING STARCH INTO SUGAR

On page 30 you were told that starch is a food and that digestive juices convert starch into sugars. Starch molecules consist of many hundreds of sugar molecules joined up in a *giant molecule*. The giant molecules of starch are broken down into the simpler sugar molecules when we chew our food, by the action of a material called *ptyalin* that is present in our saliva. Here is an experiment to show that starch is destroyed by saliva.

First make a paste with about a saltspoonful of starch and cold water. Pour on to the paste about a cupful of boiling water. When your starch solution has cooled, divide it between two glasses. Obtain a good supply of saliva by chewing a clean rubber and spit into one glass. Leave the glasses in a warm room for about fifteen minutes and then test each solution. Do this by putting two drops of iodine on to a white plate and adding to the iodine a drop of solution from each glass. The liquid from the glass with your saliva added will give little or no colour to the iodine, while the other liquid will produce the usual blue.

Germinating barley seeds also contain a substance that converts starch into sugar. This substance is called *diastase*.

Leave some barley seeds between damp blotting paper in a warm room until sprouting starts, usually after about four to six days. Then put the seeds on a block of hard wood and break them open with a hammer. Put the broken seeds into a cup and add a tablespoonful of lukewarm water to dissolve the diastase. When the undissolved material has settled, use the solution in place of saliva to destroy starch.

CHEMICAL OPPOSITES

There are two important kinds of chemical compounds that act in opposite ways. They are called ACIDS and BASES.

Anything that has a sour taste is almost sure to have an acid in it. There is lactic acid in sour milk, citric acid in lemons, and acetic acid in vinegar.

Most bases are found only in laboratory chemicals and certain drugs, but sodium bicarbonate (baking soda) acts like a base. You can use it as a base in your experiments.

Because they are opposites, acids and bases work against each other. If exactly the right amounts of an acid and a base are mixed, they will cancel each other. What is left will be like neither one. This means that the acid and the base NEUTRALIZE each other.

Chemists can tell when an acid and a base are neutralized. They put in a special chemical that changes colour when there is either too much acid or base in the mixture. A material that does this is called an INDICATOR.

Red cabbage has a compound in it that works as an indicator. Use it in an experiment.

Cut part of a head of red cabbage into small pieces. Put a full glass of water into a pan and add half a glass of cut cabbage. Bring the water to a boil, then turn the flame low and let the mixture cook about ten minutes. The liquid will turn dark red. Holding back the cabbage with a spoon, pour the liquid off into a glass and let it cool.

You can now use this liquid as an indicator. Pour some of it into a saucer. Put in about a quarter of a teaspoon of baking soda and stir. The dark red colour will change to a deep green, which shows that the baking soda made the mixture a *base*.

Now stir the liquid as you add vinegar, a little at a time. Bubbles form and the mixture flashes red where the vinegar goes in. Keep adding vinegar and stirring until all the liquid stays red. This will mean that the mixture is again *acid*.

You can change the colour back and forth several times, just by adding more baking soda or more vinegar.

The indicator shows exactly when you have just the right amount of acid and base to neutralize each other. Chemists use many other compounds as indicators to check on chemical changes.

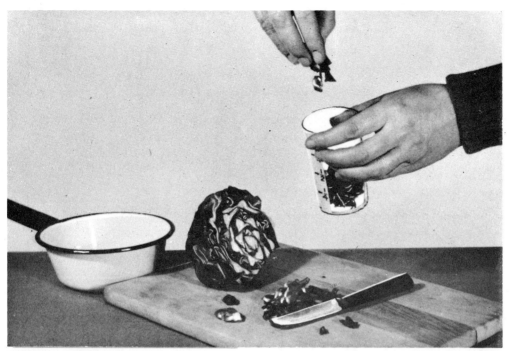

Cut the cabbage into small pieces.

Add some baking soda.

METAL FROM THE OCEAN

In the last experiment, you used an indicator to tell you when an acid and a base neutralized each other. Here is an experiment in which no indicator is needed. The base itself will change form to tell you when it is neutralized.

Put a teaspoon of Epsom salts in a quarter of a glass of water and stir until the crystals dissolve. Notice that the liquid is clear.

Add about half an inch of ammonia and stir again. The liquid begins to get cloudy. Let the glass stand for about five minutes and you will find that a white jelly forms. This material is a base called MAGNESIUM HYDROXIDE. It soon settles to the bottom of the glass.

Now pour in about half an inch of vinegar and stir. The magnesium hydroxide will begin to disappear. Add more vinegar until the liquid is completely clear again.

The acid in the vinegar neutralized the magnesium hydroxide, which is a base. When this jelly-like material disappeared, you could tell that the mixture was neutral without using an indicator.

Chemists make magnesium hydroxide come out of sea water in order to get the metal MAGNESIUM. This is the lightest of all useful metals, and so is very valuable for making automobile and aeroplane parts. There is about a pound of magnesium in the amount of sea water it would take to fill a bathtub.

Above: The liquid begins to get cloudy.
Below: Adding vinegar clears it again.

PLASTICS

You know that milk is one of the most healthful and important of all foods. It is hard to believe that chemists can change part of it into paint, glue, a kind of wool and many other things. Millions of gallons of milk are used in this way every year.

The wonderful material in milk that makes this possible is called CASEIN. You can do an experiment to get some casein out of milk.

Pour a pint of milk into an enamelled pan and heat very gently until it feels slightly warm when you dip in your finger. Take the pan off the stove. Stir the milk as you slowly pour in half a glass of vinegar. Some thick, white pieces will begin to form in the liquid.

Keep stirring the mixture until the pieces gather into a rubbery mass. Lift this out of the pan and squeeze out the liquid.

You now have casein, which is the starting point for making all sorts of objects. The chemist first gets the casein from milk, just as you did in your experiment. Then he dries it, grinds it to a powder, adds some water and colouring, and kneads it into a dough. This dough is pressed in a heated mould to give it the shape that is wanted. Then it is hardened by dipping it into a chemical liquid.

Any soft material, such as casein, that will hold its shape after it is hardened is called a PLASTIC. Chemists have discovered how to make many kinds of plastics. New and useful things are being made all the time from these shining, colourful, long-lasting materials.

Lift out the white mass.

Many things are made of plastics.

HOW SOAP WORKS

Most dirt sticks to clothes and skin because a thin layer of oil or grease holds it there. Soap is able to break up this layer so that the dirt can be floated away. An experiment will show you how soap does its work.

Put about an inch of water in a test tube. Add another inch of any kind of oil. You can use cooking oil from the kitchen or mineral oil from the medicine cabinet. Notice that the two liquids stay separated. The oil is on top and the water is below.

Put your thumb over the end of the tube and shake the liquid well. The oil will break up into drops all through the water, but in a few moments the drops will gather together again. This is because oil does not dissolve in water.

Now dissolve half a teaspoon of soap powder in half a glass of water. Pour about an inch of the soapy liquid into another test tube and add oil as before. This time, when you shake the tube you get a milky white liquid which does not separate out for a long time. It is now an EMULSION.

An emulsion is made up of tiny drops of oil or fat spread all through water. In your experiment, soap broke the oil into small drops and kept them from flowing together again. In washing, soap works by forming an emulsion with the grease that holds dirt. Water can then carry the dirt away.

Milk is an emulsion that you know well. It is made up mainly of tiny drops of fat spread through water. The fat can be separated out by churning, which knocks the drops together to form butter.

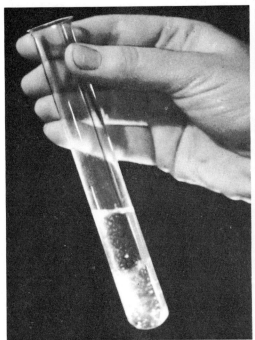
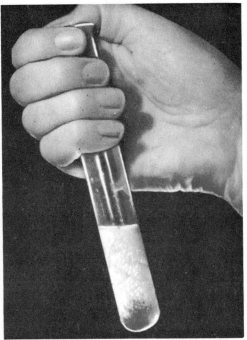

The oil and water do not mix.   Shaking does not help.

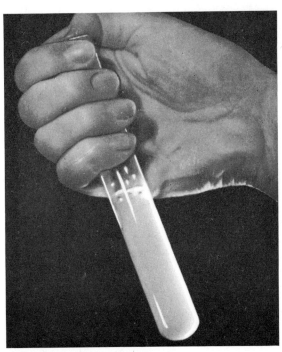

Soap lets the two liquids mix.

WATER THAT WASTES SOAP

Almost all water has some materials, called MINERALS, dissolved in it. These minerals are usually compounds of the elements calcium, magnesium or iron. They are taken up by the water as it goes through the ground. In some places, there are large amounts of minerals in the water, and this kind is called HARD water.

Soap does not lather well in hard water. The dissolved minerals join chemically with the soap before it can do its work. To see how this happens, try an experiment.

Get ready some very hard water by dissolving a teaspoon of Epsom salts in about a quarter of a glass of water. Put about the same amount of water in another glass and dissolve some soap in it.

Pour the hard water into the soapy liquid. Pieces of thick, white material form. Rub some between your fingers and notice how sticky it is. This compound has much of the soap tied up in it. The soap was used up before it could form a lather.

In your experiment, be sure to use soap and not a detergent. A detergent is a special kind of cleaning compound that is not easily weakened by the minerals in hard water.

Hard water can be made SOFT by certain chemicals. This is often done in the laundry by adding washing soda or borax to the water.

The salt water of the ocean can be made fit to drink by softening it. Sea water is pressed through a plastic bag with chemicals in it, and drinkable water comes out.

Pour the hard water into the soapy liquid.

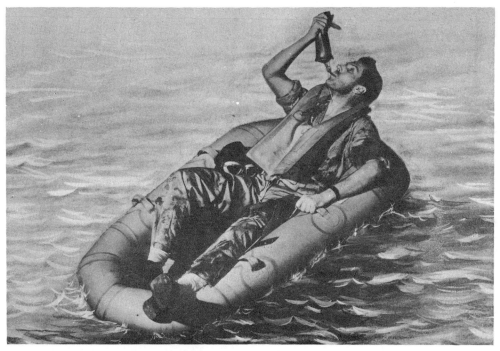

Sea water can be made drinkable.

HOW CHEMISTS USE ELECTRICITY

The electric current from a battery is kept going by chemical action. This works the opposite way, too. Chemical changes can be caused by an electric current, and that is what happens in this experiment:

Tape together two flashlight cells so that the bottom of one rests on the top post of the other. Scrape the paper cover off part of the lower cell so that the clean metal shows.

Get two short pieces of copper wire and scrape them clean as far as about two inches from each end. Twist an end of one piece of wire around the cleaned part of the cell. Wind the other end around a pencil a few times to form a curl. Make the same kind of curl on the other piece of wire.

Dissolve two teaspoons of salt in a glass of water. Fill a test tube right to the top with some of this salt water. Pour the rest into a soup plate. Using your thumb as a stopper, turn the tube upside down in the liquid in the plate. Then remove your thumb while keeping the opening of the tube under water. Do this carefully and the water will not run out of the tube.

Now, still keeping the opening of the tube under water, slide in the curled end of the wire that comes from the battery. Lay the curled end of the second wire in the salt water and hold the other end of this wire tightly against the centre post of the upper cell. The picture shows how everything should look.

You will see many small bubbles streaming off the curl of wire inside the test tube. These are bubbles of hydrogen gas that gather at the top of the tube. An electric current from the battery is now going around through the liquid. The hydrogen was set free from the water by this current.

At the other curl, an element called CHLORINE comes out of the salt. It joins chemically with the copper and gives the wire a dull covering.

After the current has been on for a little while, you will notice that the liquid becomes slightly blue. This colour is from copper atoms that came off the wire.

All these chemical changes were caused by the electric current going through the liquid.

Chlorine is a very useful chemical element. It is made in huge tanks in about the same way as in your experiment.

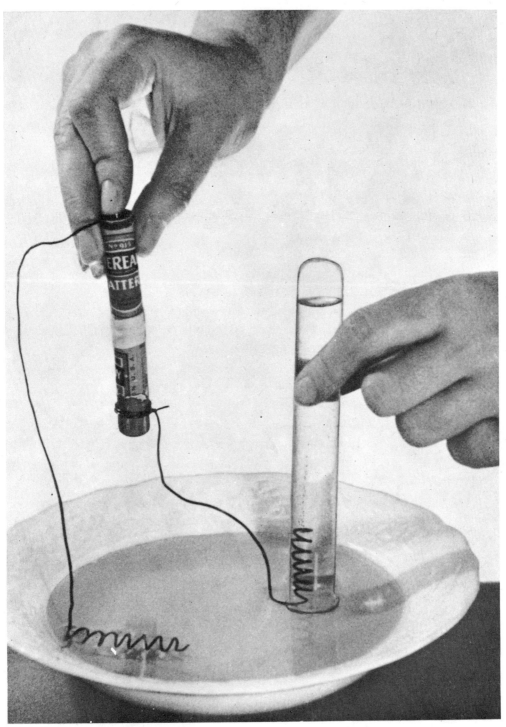

A gas gathers at the top of the tube.

BREATHING PLANTS

If you were to ask a chemist what he thought was the most important chemical action in the world, he would be almost sure to answer, 'The making of starch and sugar by plants.'

A green plant is nature's chemical laboratory. Plants can take carbon dioxide from the air and join it to water from the soil to make starch and sugar. They are able to do this because of the action of sunlight on the green colouring material of the leaves. Chemists have not yet found how to make this action go on without the help of plants.

Get a small growing plant, such as ivy or some other vine. Fill a test tube to the very top with water. Use your thumb as a stopper and turn the tube upside down in a bowl of water. Carefully keep the opening of the tube under water as you take your thumb away and push an end of the plant up into the tube, as in the picture. Put the whole set-up out in the sun.

After a few hours, you will see a space at the top of the tube. This space is filled with oxygen which was set free when sunlight fell on the leaves of the plant.

The growing ivy takes up carbon dioxide and water and builds them into starch and sugar. When this happens, oxygen is set free and comes out of the leaves. In your experiment, you caught the oxygen that came from the leaves inside the test tube.

As you watch this chemical change happen, remember that there could be no life on earth without it. That is because everything that lives is either a plant or an animal that needs plants for food.

Getting oxygen from a growing plant.

LIGHT BREAKS DOWN MOLECULES

The last experiment showed that light can build up compounds. It can help break down some compounds, too.

Whenever you take a picture with your camera, you are using light to cause chemical changes. Rays of light from the scene you want to photograph go through the lens of the camera. They hit the film and change some of the special compounds on it. The film is then taken out of the camera in the darkroom and put through chemical liquids to bring out the picture.

You can use light to make pictures without a camera or film.

Lay a sheet of bright-coloured poster paper in strong sunlight. Get some flat objects such as a key, a coin, a pair of scissors and a paper clip, and lay them on the paper. Cut your initials out of cardboard and put them down there, too.

After a considerable time, depending on the weather, take the things off the paper and you will see their exact shadow pictures.

Wherever it was not covered, the paper lost some of its colour. This was because the rays of the sun broke down the molecules of the dye.

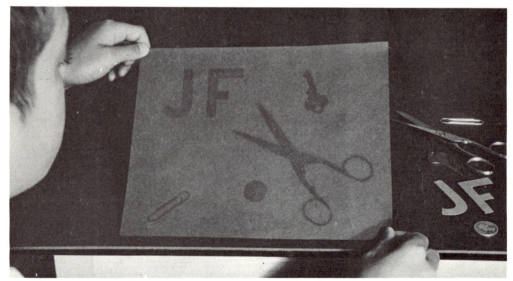

Shadow pictures are left on the paper.

58